Primary Ecology Series

The Air I Breathe

Bobbie Kalman & Janine Schaub

Crabtree Publishing Company

The Primary Ecology Series
Created by Bobbie Kalman

For Halley Ann Schaub

Writing team
Bobbie Kalman
Janine Schaub

Editor-in-chief
Bobbie Kalman

Editors
David Schimpky
Shelagh Wallace

Design and computer layout
Antoinette "Cookie" DeBiasi

Artwork and cover design
Antoinette "Cookie" DeBiasi
Illustration page 13: Jeff Pykerman

Cover mechanicals
Rose Campbell

Separations and film
EC Graphics

Printer
Worzalla Publishing

Photographs:
Bobbie Kalman (with Antoinette DeBiasi):
Cover (front and back), title page, pages 4, 5
(right), 8, 9, 25, 26, 27
Diane Payton Majumdar: pages 5 (left), 16, 20
Ursula Osborn: page 18

Special thanks to: Christina Doyle, Maria
Picard, Bill McBride, Joy Furminger, Andy
Osborn, Samantha Crabtree (on cover and
title page), The Cancer Society, the students
of Michael J. Brennan and Pine Grove
Elementary Schools: Brian Bell, Darrick Yu,
Myroslawa Tataryn, Kelvin Bascus, Hilary
Kuzmaski, Erin Yurenko, Darcia Fraser,
Stacey Baugaard, Laura Zapata, Jonathan
Lau, Stacey Langelaan, Paul Hammond, and
Ehi Idahosa

Published by
Crabtree Publishing Company

350 Fifth Avenue	360 York Road, RR4,	73 Lime Walk
Suite 3308	Niagara-on-the-Lake,	Headington
New York	Ontario, Canada	Oxford OX3 7AD
N.Y. 10118	L0S 1J0	United Kingdom

Cataloguing in Publication Data
Kalman, Bobbie, 1947-
  The air I breathe

(The Primary ecology series)
Includes index.
ISBN 0-86505-556-4 (library bound) ISBN 0-86505-582-3 (pbk.)
This book explores the importance of air to all living things, how
weather is made, and how air pollution threatens the earth.

1. Air - Juvenile literature. 2. Respiration - Juvenile literature.
3. Weather - Juvenile literature.
4. Air - Pollution - Juvenile literature.
I. Schaub, Janine II. Title III. Series: The Primary ecology series

QC161.2.K35 1993   j551.5   LC 93-30693

Contents

❧ The breath of life ❧

...fifty-eight, fifty-nine, sixty! Even when you have practiced holding your breath, you can only last a minute or so without gasping for air. People, like all plants and animals, need air to survive. We cannot live without it for more than a few minutes! Air is made up of a mixture of invisible gases. These gases cover the surface of the earth like a blanket and make our planet the only one in our solar system that is able to support life.

Invisible air

Although we cannot see or smell air, we can feel moving air touching us on a windy day. Cold winter air can swirl around us and make us shiver. A hot breeze on a summer day can send us in search of a cooler spot.

Air can carry smells, tiny particles, or even large objects. We can see dust, fog, or smoke in the air. Airplanes, kites, birds, and frisbees are also familiar objects that we can see flying through the air.

The uses of air

Each day we use air in many different ways. Air heats and cools us. We dry our clothes and hair with it. Air allows us to sail boats and fly airplanes.

It creates beautiful sounds when we blow it through some musical instruments.

Air carries the seeds of plants to places where they can grow. When it is trapped between fur or feathers, air keeps animals and birds warm.

Air can be used as a source of energy. It turns windmills. The energy from a turning windmill produces electricity to power machines and appliances.

Air is great!

We don't think about air because it is invisible and we have so much of it, but it is nature's most important gift to us. Can you think of some other ways in which we use air?

Air helps carry seeds to where they can grow.

Air helps us make beautiful music!

❦ Our bodies need air ❦

Sit down and close your eyes. Feel the air around your face and body. Visualize air entering your nostrils and filling your lungs. Feel the air leaving your nostrils again. Take a deep breath and, this time, picture the air reaching every cell of your body. As you are breathing in, think about how precious each breath is to you.

Inhaling and exhaling

In order to survive, we need air. Our bodies need energy for running and playing. We get this energy from the air we breathe and the food we eat. Each time we breathe in, or **inhale**, we take in a gas called **oxygen**. Oxygen is one of the gases that makes up air. After oxygen is used by our bodies, a waste gas called **carbon dioxide** is made. Our bodies get rid of this gas each time we breathe out, or **exhale**.

How we breathe

Each day you take in thousands of breaths. Without thinking about it, you breathe in and out about fifteen times every minute. If you are chasing a ball or playing tag, you breathe a lot faster.

Into the lungs

When you take a big breath, the air travels down your throat through your **windpipe**. The windpipe branches off into two tubes. Each tube goes to one of your two **lungs**. Lungs are big pink sacs that contain many blood vessels.

Carried by your blood

When air enters your lungs, oxygen is passed into your blood and pumped all over your body by your heart. The carbon dioxide in your body is then carried by your blood back to your lungs and is ready to be exhaled.

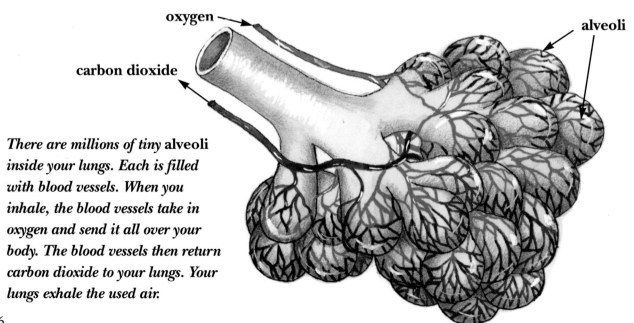

oxygen

carbon dioxide

alveoli

There are millions of tiny alveoli inside your lungs. Each is filled with blood vessels. When you inhale, the blood vessels take in oxygen and send it all over your body. The blood vessels then return carbon dioxide to your lungs. Your lungs exhale the used air.

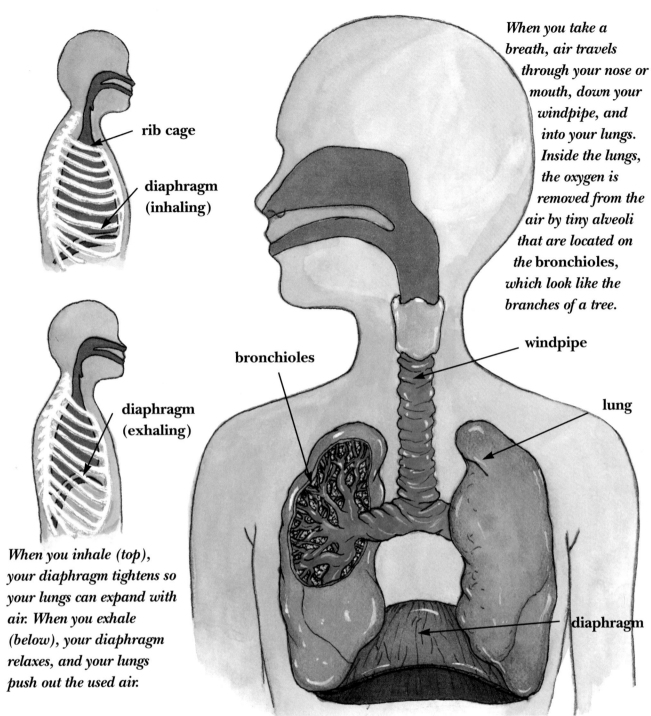

rib cage

diaphragm
(inhaling)

diaphragm
(exhaling)

When you take a breath, air travels through your nose or mouth, down your windpipe, and into your lungs. Inside the lungs, the oxygen is removed from the air by tiny alveoli that are located on the bronchioles, which look like the branches of a tree.

bronchioles

windpipe

lung

diaphragm

When you inhale (top), your diaphragm tightens so your lungs can expand with air. When you exhale (below), your diaphragm relaxes, and your lungs push out the used air.

Tighten that diaphragm!

When you take a breath of air, a big muscle under your lungs, called the **diaphragm**, tightens up. The tightened diaphragm makes the space inside your chest bigger. The air that you inhale rushes in to fill this space. When the diaphragm relaxes, used air is pushed out of the lungs.

Your ribs form a cage of bones that protects your lungs. Although you cannot touch your lungs or your diaphragm, you can feel your rib cage work as you breathe. When you take a deep breath, your rib cage moves upwards and outwards. Put your hands on your ribs and feel them expand.

7

❧ Power breathing ❧

Everyone breathes without thinking about it, but many people learn to breathe more efficiently. Singers and actors practice breathing control so they can sing and speak without being short of breath. Musicians who play wind instruments practice breathing to increase the amount of air they can take into their lungs. Athletes learn to breathe properly to have more energy. Women who are having babies breathe in a way that helps decrease their pain. Some people take deep breaths in an effort to control their anger.

Every breath counts!

To learn how to control their breath, some people practice deep breathing. They train their lungs to take in more air and learn how to breathe out all their stale air. People who practice this type of breathing claim that it makes them feel healthier and more energetic. Try the following exercises over a period of a few days or weeks and see if you feel better.

1. Sit on the floor with your legs tucked under you, straighten your back, and hold your head up. Close your eyes and think about breathing.

2. Count to two as you inhale. You will know that you are using your diaphragm correctly if you feel your stomach expand as you take a breath. Hold your breath and count to eight.

3. Exhale your used air slowly through your nose to the count of four. As you exhale, pull in your stomach to push out every bit of carbon dioxide from the bottom of your lungs.

4. Repeat this breathing exercise ten times and concentrate on your breath. If you begin to feel dizzy, stop and practice again later.

After doing these breathing exercises over a period of a few days, you will be able to increase your counts to 4 in, 16 hold, and 8 exhale. Try doubling those counts after several weeks of practice.

(opposite) Practice deep breathing outdoors if you can. Doing it near some trees will allow you to breathe cleaner air and make you feel as if your breath is a part of nature.

(right) To get air into the very top part of your lungs, raise your elbows over your head, as shown in the photograph, and inhale until you feel the air go all the way up your back to the shoulder area. When you exhale, push out all the carbon dioxide until you feel the tips of your lungs empty right out. Once you have practiced deep breathing using these postures, you will be able to control your breath naturally in any position.

🥀 Air lets you hear 🥀

The sounds we hear are carried by moving air. When a mouse scurries across your path, her motions move the air around her. Tiny particles of moving air travel in a wave similar to the way a ripple is made by throwing a pebble into a pond. When the air wave caused by the mouse reaches your ears, you hear a scurrying sound.

Rainbows of ripples

Each day we hear all kinds of sounds traveling through the air in waves. Radio and television stations send their signals out as air waves.

Cellular phone calls and microwaves are sent through the air in waves, too. If air waves had colors, the sky would be filled with rainbows of ripples.

Send an air wave

Stretch a piece of tissue paper over one end of a paper tube and hold it in place with a rubber band. Put your mouth up to the open end and talk into the tube. Place your finger gently on the surface of the paper at the other end. You will feel the air waves that have been sent out by your own voice as the paper vibrates.

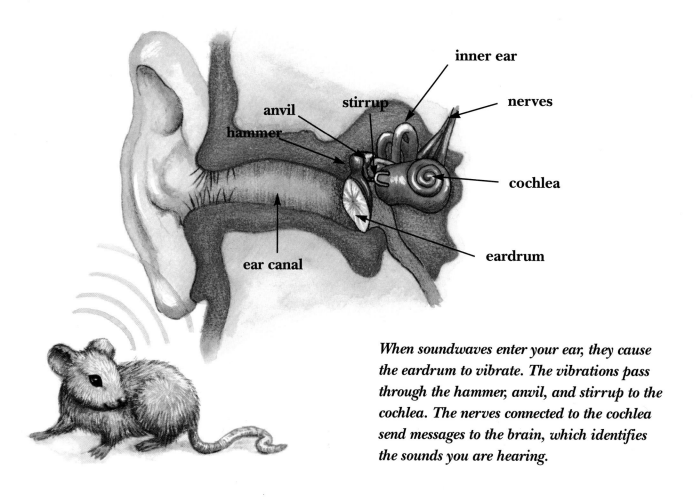

When soundwaves enter your ear, they cause the eardrum to vibrate. The vibrations pass through the hammer, anvil, and stirrup to the cochlea. The nerves connected to the cochlea send messages to the brain, which identifies the sounds you are hearing.

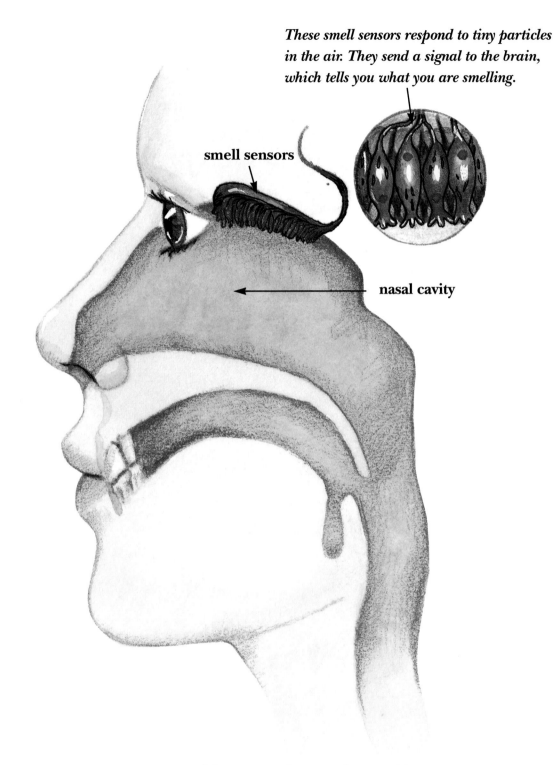

These smell sensors respond to tiny particles in the air. They send a signal to the brain, which tells you what you are smelling.

smell sensors

nasal cavity

❦ Smelling the air ❦

When someone peels an orange, you can smell its fruity scent right away. Tiny drops of oil from the peel squirt out and are carried by the air to your nose. Orange-peel oil and other substances in the air make up **odors**.

Odors floating in the air enter your nostrils and travel up to a place behind the bridge of your nose. It is in that spot that your nose detects odors. The smell information is then passed to your brain, which identifies the odor.

The journey of air

A hot-air balloon can float because the warm air inside it is lighter than the cool, heavy air that surrounds the balloon. Just as the hot air in the balloon makes the balloon rise, air also rises when it is heated by the sun. Cooler air then rushes in to take its place. When cool and warm air change places, the result is wind.

Air never leaves the earth

Air is forever circling our planet. The frosty wind that swirled around a boy who lives in the Arctic may now be blowing past you. That same mass of air may then move farther south and bring rain to a village in the Caribbean. Later this year, that same air might again blow through your hair as a warm, gentle breeze. Although air travels all over the planet, it never leaves the atmosphere!

You are the wind!

Imagine following the air that you just exhaled. Picture yourself soaring across the ocean and see your breath become a gust of wind. Follow that gust as it joins a cool mountain breeze. Trail the breeze through a rain forest where the leaves of the trees cleanse and moisten it. Watch the fresh air blow back across the land, ready for you to breathe again. Inhale the clean air and become part of the wind!

Imagine you are a part of the wind!

🍂 Wind is moving air 🍂

When the wind blows, air is moving from place to place. Sometimes wind gently rustles leaves. On stormy days the wind can be strong enough to knock down trees.

Some winds blow because there is a difference in the temperatures on land and on the sea. Air above land gets hot faster and rises. Cooler air from above the ocean then moves in to take its place.

Which way does it blow?
Wind usually means that the weather is changing. Weather forecasters are interested in the direction of the wind because it helps them predict the type of weather that is on its way.

The windchill factor
On windy winter days, weather forecasters often tell people how cold it is by reporting two different temperatures. The first is the actual temperature outside. The second temperature is a measure of how cold the air feels with the wind blowing. When it is cold and windy outside, the air swirls around you and cools down your body. This effect is called the **windchill factor**. It can make a cold day feel even colder. Brrr!

Mighty winds
Some high-speed winds are strong enough to toss streetcars and knock down buildings! Strong winds are part of huge tropical storms called **hurricanes** and whirling spirals called **tornadoes**.

A hurricane is on its way!
Hurricanes begin as small thunderstorms over warm oceans. Several storms cluster and start swirling towards land. They bring huge waves, raging winds, and heavy rain that may last many hours.

Funnels of destruction
Tornadoes are spinning funnels of wind that are created inside storm clouds during a thunderstorm. These tight funnels hang down from the clouds and suck up everything in their path. They last only a few minutes but cause a great deal of destruction wherever they touch the ground.

How strong is the wind?

Many years ago, a man called Beaufort developed a scale to measure the speed of the wind. As the wind blew, he carefully observed what objects it was able to move. On days with little or no wind, he gave the wind speed a code number of zero. On the stormiest days, he gave the wind speed a code number of 12. Beaufort's observations were all made at sea. The Beaufort Scale in the box below has been changed to include observations on land. Using the chart below as a guide, write your own wind observations on a piece of paper. Check them against the chart at the bottom of this page. What number did you assign to the strongest wind you observed?

Wind observations	Code number (the force of the wind)
leaves rustle	1-2
(your observations)	3-4
(your observations)	5-6
(your observations)	7-8
(your observations)	9-10
trees are uprooted	11
buildings are destroyed	12

The Beaufort Scale

Number	Title	Wind effect
0	calm	Smoke goes straight up.
1	light air	Smoke drifts in the direction of the wind.
2	light breeze	Flags flutter; leaves rustle.
3	gentle breeze	Flags blow straight out; small branches move.
4	moderate breeze	Dust and papers blow around.
5	fresh breeze	Whitecaps appear on water; small trees bend in the wind.
6	strong breeze	Large branches move; umbrellas turn inside out.
7	high wind	Whole trees bend. You have to lean against the wind in order to move.
8	gale	Small branches break off trees.
9	strong gale	Signs blow down; shingles blow off rooftops.
10	storm	Trees fall and wires and light structures blow down.
11	violent storm	Trees are uprooted. There is widespread damage.
12	hurricane	Buildings, cars, and boats are destroyed.

❧ Thunder and lightning ❧

Does your pet hide under your bed during a thunderstorm? Have you ever been so scared that you have climbed into your parents' bed?

Although thunder sounds scary, it is not caused by a frightening event at all. Crashes of thunder are created by moving air.

Zap!

If you have ever been zapped by a small shock from a fuzzy blanket, you know what **static electricity** feels like. Static electricity also forms inside huge, black, billowy clouds called **thunderclouds**. When air moves very quickly up and down inside thunderclouds, it smashes water droplets and ice crystals against one another. All this activity causes a great deal of static electricity to build up and make a giant spark called **lightning**.

Kinds of lightning

Lightning can occur within a single cloud, shoot between two clouds, or jump from a cloud to the earth. **Forked lightning** is the crooked lightning that zigzags across the sky. **Ball lightning** looks like balloons of fire that explode when they hit the ground. **Sheet lightning** lights up the whole sky.

Crack or rumble?

If you happen to be at the center of a thunderstorm, you will see lightning flash and hear thunder crack at almost the same instant. If you are some distance away from the storm, the rumble of thunder will follow shortly after the lightning flashes. Light travels through air much more quickly than sound does. That is why there is a delay before you hear thunder.

Thunder countdown

To find out how close you are to a thunderstorm, count the number of seconds between a lightning flash and its thunder. A delay of three seconds means that the storm is only 1.6 kilometers (one mile) away.

Thunderstorm caution

It is very unlikely that you will ever be struck by lightning, but thunderstorms can be dangerous if you are caught outdoors. Play it safe by following these suggestions:

- If you are swimming outdoors, get out of the water and go indoors, if possible.
- If you are caught outdoors, avoid high ground. Lightning often uses the tallest object available to find an easy path to the ground. Lie flat on low-level ground.
- Keep away from tall trees and lone boulders.
- Stay away from large metal structures and do not hold onto metal objects such as fences.
- If you are in a car, stay there. The rubber tires on a car will help protect you if lightning strikes.
- If you have an antenna on your roof, unplug your television set.

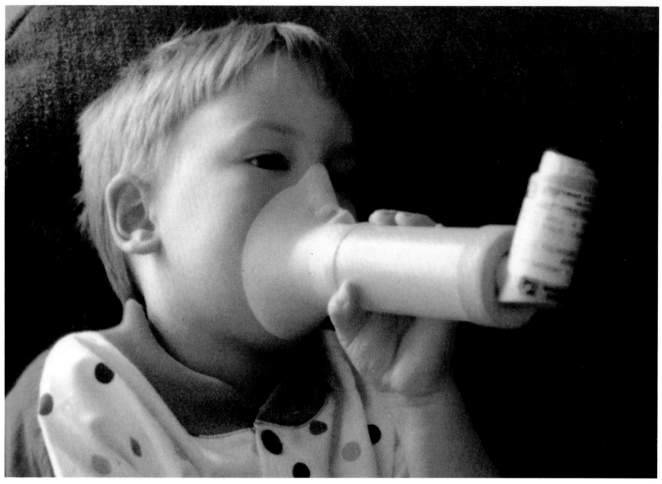

🌿 Shared air 🌿

You share many things in your classroom. You share the space around you with your classmates. You share school supplies, books, and ideas. You might even share your lunch with a friend. One of the most important things you share, however, is air! Some of the air in your lungs right now has already been in the lungs of every other person in the same room.

Unhealthy air

The inside of your nose is coated with a wet, sticky substance called **mucus**. Most of the time, this mucus traps dirt and germs in the air before they get into our lungs. If the air is poisoned or very dirty, however, mucus cannot stop all the pollution from reaching the lungs. Once pollution is inside the lungs, it can cause damage and make you sick.

Allergies and asthma

People with **allergies** are very sensitive to some substances in the air. Dust, pollution, and pollen from plants can cause people to cough and sneeze. People suffering from allergies often have runny noses and watery eyes. Sometimes allergies cause an illness called **asthma**. The breathing tubes inside the body become swollen, making it difficult to get enough air.

Lung diseases and cancer

Many people suffer from lung diseases. Harmful smoke, gases, and chemicals in the air damage people's lungs. People with sick lungs or growths in their lungs, called **cancers**, can become very ill and even die.

Smoking

Tobacco smoke contains many poisonous substances that make people's lungs dirty. It clogs the lungs with sticky black tar. Smoking is not only dangerous to the health of the smoker, but also to the people around the smoker. In fact, scientists have found that second-hand smoke inhaled by non-smokers is even more poisonous than smoke that is inhaled directly from a cigarette. Smoking eventually destroys the lungs. It also damages the heart, arteries, mouth, and throat of a smoker.

Demand clean air!

Do you know someone who smokes? Does that person smoke when he or she is in the same room as you are? The next time this happens, tell that person that you do not wish to have your lungs damaged and ask him or her to respect your wish to breathe clean air. Stick up for your rights and your lungs and make a decision never to start smoking!

(opposite) Andy uses an inhaler when he has an asthma attack. Without it, he would find it very difficult to breathe. (below) Healthy lungs, such as the ones on the left, are pink and shiny. A smoker's lungs, on the right, are dark gray and dull. Many people who smoke get emphysema or cancer. Both diseases can cause death.

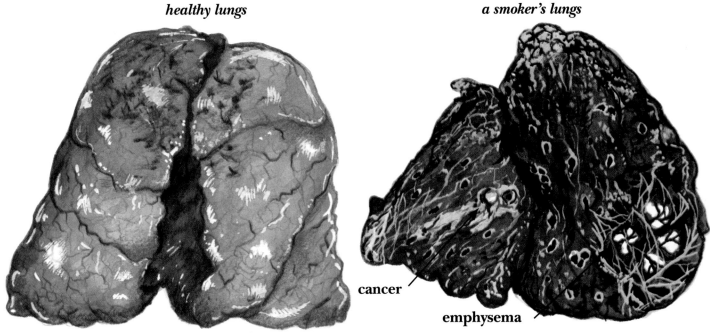

healthy lungs

a smoker's lungs

cancer

emphysema

❦ Air pollution ❦

When we take a breath, we inhale the air around us. Most of the time that air is clean enough to breathe but, sometimes, it is dirty with **pollution**.

Air pollution is caused by chemicals and gases in the air that should not be there. Air pollution is harmful to all plants, animals, and people.

Car exhaust

Cars and other vehicles that use fuel create air pollution. When fuels such as gasoline or diesel are burned inside car engines, they give the car the power to move. The waste gas from burned fuel comes out of the tail pipe. This gas is called **exhaust**, and it is poisonous to living things.

Smog

In some cities of the world the air is polluted with **smog**. The exhaust from cars and smoke from factories mixes with moist air and sunlight. Smog covers many cities in a blanket of brownish, bad-smelling fog. In many cities, such as Mexico City, some people wear special masks to try to protect their lungs from the smog.

Household pollution

Some of the cleaning products we use in our homes can cause air pollution. Oven cleaners use a chemical called **ammonia**, which is harmful to our lungs. Many paints, thinners, and glues allow dangerous chemicals to escape into the air. Some beauty products, such as nail polish and hair spray, also pollute the air. Many families are now choosing to use safe products that do not pollute the air or water. Is your family careful about using environmentally friendly products?

Smoke

When forests burn or volcanoes erupt, smoke is sent into the air. Volcanoes and burning forests pollute the air, but most of the smoke that dirties our air is made by people. Factories make smoke that is filled with dangerous chemicals. Although many smoke-stacks are fitted with devices that reduce pollution, a lot of poisons still escape into the air.

The greenhouse effect

Have you ever been in a greenhouse? Was it hot? The glass, roof, and walls of a greenhouse trap the sun's heat, making greenhouses uncomfortably warm when the sun shines. In a similar way, carbon dioxide can build up in the atmosphere and trap heat. The result of this trapped heat is called the **greenhouse effect** or **global warming**.

Deadly to all life

Global warming can be deadly to the earth. If the temperature of the earth becomes just a few degrees warmer, plants will dry out and forests will die. The ice at the North and South poles will melt and raise the water level of the oceans. The oceans will then flood many coastal areas where millions of people live.

❧ Layers of air ❧

The few kilometers of air that surround the earth make our planet different from any other planet in the solar system. This blanket of air allows all living things to survive. Its special balance of gases keeps the planet alive, like one large breathing body. Air connects us to water, plants, animals, and other human beings. It is something we all need and share.

Blast-off!

You are boarding the space shuttle and preparing yourself for a trip through the layers of air that make up the earth's **atmosphere**. You blast off and, in seconds, you've passed through the thin band of breathable air that surrounds the planet. The ride is bumpy as you rocket past clouds and burst into the still, clear layers of the upper atmosphere.

Outside, the air is no longer cool but scorching hot. You look out your window and see several whitish-blue bands of air meeting dark sky. You get butterflies in your stomach as you realize that you are leaving your planet and entering outer space!

Through the atmosphere

The **troposphere** is the layer of air closest to the earth. It is the layer in which we live and where weather is formed. Airplanes fly at the top of the troposphere, where the air is calm.

The **stratosphere** is next. The **ozone layer** is part of this band of air. The ozone layer shields the earth from the harmful rays of the sun.

The **mesosphere** is the coldest layer of the atmosphere. Meteorites that are pulled towards the earth by gravity break apart here.

The **thermosphere** is five times as deep as all the other layers of the atmosphere put together. The sun can raise the temperature in this layer to a sizzling 2000°C (3600°F).

Communication satellites circle the earth in the thermosphere and **exosphere**. They pick up signals and allow people all over the world to communicate by radio, television, and telephone.

The exosphere fades into black space. The pull of gravity is gone.

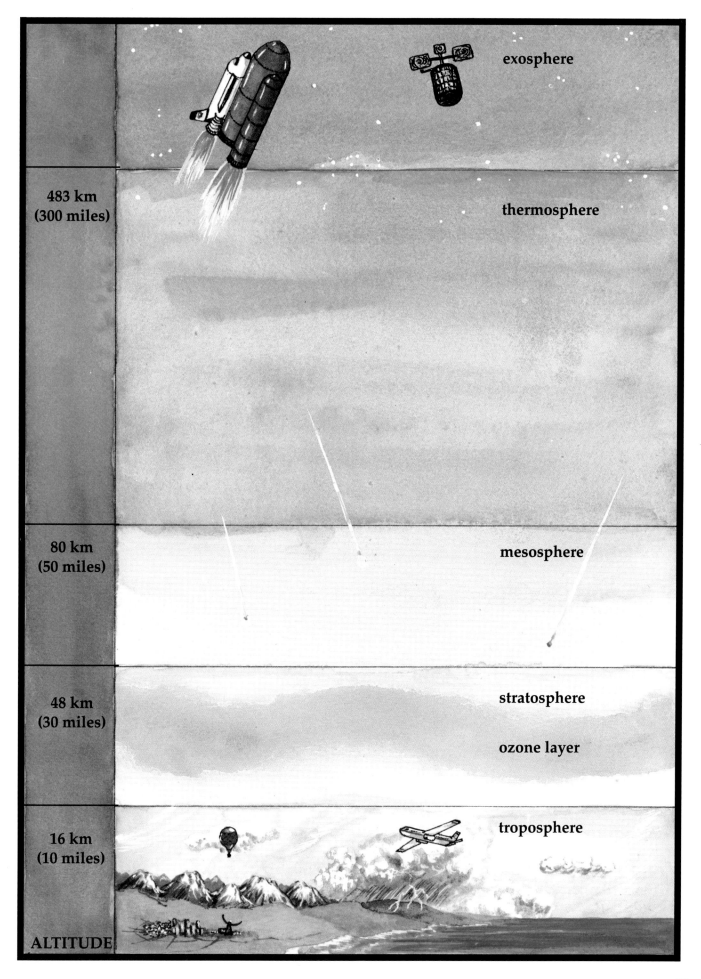

ALTITUDE

	exosphere
483 km (300 miles)	thermosphere
80 km (50 miles)	mesosphere
48 km (30 miles)	stratosphere
	ozone layer
16 km (10 miles)	troposphere

❦ Bad ozone, good ozone ❦

There are two types of ozone. **Ground ozone**, found near the earth's surface, is bad ozone. It is a type of air pollution. It comes from car exhaust and chemical fumes that are heated by the sun. When ground ozone is in the air we breathe, it irritates people's eyes and skin and can permanently damage the lungs. Ground ozone is also harmful to crops and forests.

Good ozone

Good ozone is a bluish gas found high up in the stratosphere. It covers the earth like a thin blanket 13 to 48 kilometers (8 to 30 miles) above the earth. The ozone layer stops most of the sun's ultraviolet rays from reaching the ground.

The thinning ozone

The ozone layer is being worn away by chemicals. In 1985 a hole was found above Antarctica at the South Pole. Since then, tests show that the hole is now more than four times as large, and the ozone layer is also thinning rapidly above the North Pole. New holes may soon appear over areas where millions of people live.

Harmful CFCs

The ozone layer is being destroyed by chemicals called **chlorofluorocarbons (CFCs)** that are still in use today. CFCs can be found in the cooling fluids used in refrigerators and air conditioners, in plastic-foam cartons, and in some spray cans.

The ozone layer protects the earth from harmful radiation, but ground ozone hurts plants, animals, and people.

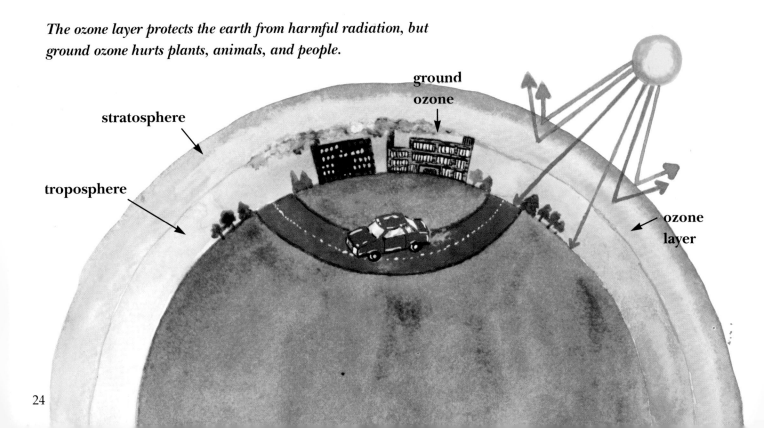

stratosphere

troposphere

ground ozone

ozone layer

Ultraviolet damage

Ultraviolet rays turn our skin darker, but they can also give us sunburns, wrinkles, skin cancer, and **cataracts**. A cataract is a clouding of the eye that causes blurred vision and blindness.

Ultraviolet rays weaken our **immune system**. A strong immune system helps us fight off diseases. Ultraviolet rays also destroy plants and animals and threaten the world's food supply.

Protect your skin from the dangerous rays of the sun by following these suggestions:

• Do not spend time in the direct sun between 10 am and 3 pm. If you have to be outdoors, stay in the shade as much as possible.

• Wear a wide-brimmed hat that protects the tips of your ears and the back of your neck from the sun's rays. Wear a long-sleeved shirt and long pants to shield your arms and legs from the sun.

• Use a sunscreen with a protection factor of at least 15 on your face and any part of your body that is not covered by clothing.

• Do not choose sunglasses just because they look good. Buy ones that block ultraviolet rays. Ordinary dark lenses that have not been treated to absorb the sun's harmful rays will damage your eyes. These dark lenses cause your pupils to open up, or **dilate**, letting in even more ultraviolet light than when you are not wearing sunglasses at all!

❧ Cleaning the air ❧

Raindrops and snowflakes help clean the air. As they fall through the sky, they catch little bits of dirt and dust that float in the air and carry them to the earth. These particles of dirt and dust then become part of the soil or sink to the bottom of lakes and oceans.

Keep it green!

Plants are great at freshening the air. They filter air through their leaves. Filtering removes some of the floating dirt. Some household plants, such as the spider plant, are especially good at this job.

Oxygen makers

Besides cleaning the air, the plants and trees that cover our earth carry out an even more important job—they help balance the gases in our air by using up carbon dioxide and making oxygen.

Green plants use sunlight, water, and carbon dioxide to make their food, and while they are making their food, they give off oxygen. By planting trees and other kinds of plants, we can help clean the air we breathe.

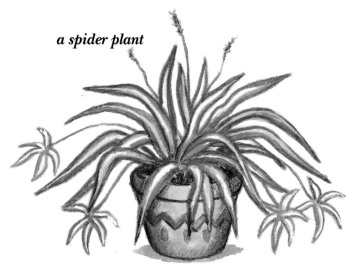
a spider plant

Plants in the classroom

Do you have plants growing in your classroom? If not, ask your teacher if your class can grow some. Not only will the plants make your room look more cheerful, but they will also help keep the air fresh.

Let's have clean air!

Today people are finding ways to reduce air pollution. Some choose to ride bicycles instead of using their cars. Many people refuse to buy products that create pollution when they are manufactured or used. What steps has your family taken to reduce air pollution?

(opposite) These children like looking after the plants in their school because they know that plants help freshen the air. (below) They ride their bikes to school because bicycles do not pollute the air.

❦ Fun with air ❦

Dancing in the wind

Some gymnasts do dance routines using wands with long pieces of colorful cloth attached. As they leap through the air, the material on the wand twists and circles around them in beautiful patterns.

To make your own wand, tape long pieces of crepe-paper ribbon to a ruler. Go outside and create your own routine by making graceful swirls through the air with your wand.

Oxygen under water

If your school has an aquarium with plants growing in the water, you can watch oxygen being made. Carefully put a clean glass jar over one of the water plants. Make sure that no air is trapped inside the jar. You will notice little streams of bubbles rising from the plant. These bubbles will collect and make a space at the top of the jar. This space is filled with oxygen. Water plants release oxygen into water just as land plants give off oxygen into the air.

Keys in the breeze

Ask your family and friends for their old keys. Once you have collected fourteen keys, you can begin to make your own wind chime.

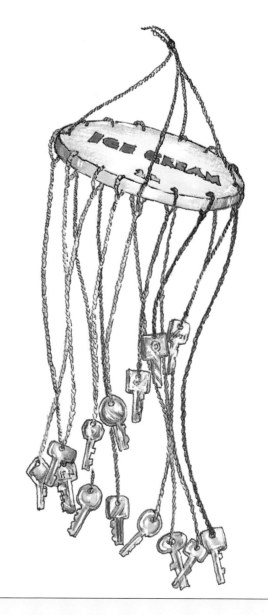

• Get an adult to help you poke fourteen holes evenly around the edge of a plastic margarine or ice-cream container lid.

• Cut fourteen pieces of string at different lengths, as shown. Insert the strings through the holes and tie them.

• Attach the old keys to the ends of the strings and hang your wind chime outside, using four pieces of string.

You will be pleased by the tinkling noise your wind chime of keys will make in the breeze!

Air sayings

We use the word "air" in many different sayings. See if you can match an air saying from List A with its meaning in List B. Write your answers on a piece of paper, not in the book.

List A	List B
1. airing out	a. pretending to be better than others
2. walking on air	b. broadcasting by radio or television
3. needing some air	c. leaving a room because you need to calm down
4. up in the air	d. being very happy
5. on the air	e. traveling or sending something by plane
6. putting on airs	f. when something is uncertain
7. by air	g. freshening up a room

🍎 A celebration of clean air 🍎

No one in my home smokes. We like our air clean! *Atef*

Air pollution makes my asthma worse. I hope people stop polluting the air. *Klara*

Spider plants help clean the air. Three cheers for spider plants! *Nutan*

Everything needs to breathe, so let's keep our air fresh! *Nicholas*

Our family rides bicycles. Bikes do not pollute the air the way cars do. *Adrienne*

Atef's grade three class is working on a project called "A celebration of clean air." Everyone has worked extra hard to finish a colorful kite to fly at the school ecology fair.

Each student has written "I like clean air" messages on ribbons. The ribbons have been attached to the tail of the kite. Read the messages on the kite's tail. What messages would you add?

❦ Glossary ❦

allergy A physical reaction, such as sneezing, to something in the air, such as pollen, dust, or pollution

ammonia A strong-smelling chemical used in some household cleaners

asthma A condition, often caused by allergies, that causes a tightness in the chest, difficulty breathing, and wheezing

atmosphere The layer of air that surrounds the earth

Beaufort Scale A scale invented by Sir Francis Beaufort that measures the force of the wind on a scale of 1 to 12

cancer A disease that can be caused by smoking

carbon dioxide A gas exhaled by humans and animals and absorbed by plants

cataracts A clouding of the eye so that light cannot get through, causing blurred vision and blindness

chlorofluorocarbons (CFCs) The chemicals that are primarily responsible for destroying the ozone layer

diaphragm A muscle in the body that separates the chest and the abdomen

ecology The relationship between living things and the environment in which they live

exhaust The poisonous fumes that escape from a car's tail pipe

global warming The theory that the earth is getting warmer because of pollution

gravity The force that pulls things towards earth

greenhouse effect See global warming

ground ozone A type of air pollution that comes from car exhaust and other fumes

hurricane A violent tropical storm of rain, lightning, thunder, and high winds

lightning The flash of light produced by static electricity in a cloud, between clouds, or between a cloud and the ground

lungs Organs in the chest used for breathing

mucus A thick, slimy body fluid found in the nose and throat

oxygen A colorless, tasteless, odorless gas in the air necessary for breathing

ozone layer The part of the atmosphere that shields the earth from the harmful rays of the sun

pollen The powdery grains of flowering plants

pollution Something that makes the environment impure or dirty

pupil The part of the eye that opens and closes to allow light to enter

rib cage The bony wall of the chest that protects the heart and lungs

satellite A human-made object placed in space to orbit the earth or moon

smog A mixture of smoke and fog

solar system The sun and all the planets and moons that revolve around it

thunder The sound following lightning that is caused by the sudden expansion of air

tornado A violent, funnel-shaped windstorm that destroys everything in its path

ultraviolet light The light from the sun that is harmful to living things

windchill factor A way of measuring temperature by including the effect of the wind

windpipe The part of the human throat that carries air to the lungs

❦ Index ❦

3 4 5 6 7 8 9 0 Printed in the U.S.A. 2 1 0 9 8 7 6 5